Amazon Fire HD 8 with Alexa:

2018 Simple User Guide How To Use All Your New Fire HD Tablet With Alexa

Alexa Embury

ISBN: 1986796280
ISBN-13: 978-1986796286

CONTENTS

Thank you for purchasing this book!

We always try to give more value then you expect. That's why we've updated the content and you can get it for FREE. You can get the digital version for free because you bought the print version.

The book is under the match program from Amazon. You can find how to do this using next URL: https://www.amazon.com/gp/digital/ep-landing-page

I hope it will be useful for you.

Introduction

Since the release of the very first device, the Fire HD tablets have been best sellers for a variety of reasons. Not only are they full of different functions, they are lightweight and affordable.

The Amazon Fire HD Tablet, like most of Amazon's products, has evolved greatly since its inception. 2017 welcomed in a new and improved generation of the tablet. The 7th generation was released in two variations, Fire HD 8 and the Fire HD 10. Jam-packed with new features and even the integration of the ever-popular assistant, Alexa, these devices are worth the purchase. This book will cover all the information you need for getting started with your brand new or potentially used Fire HD 8. The Fire HD comes fully equipped with not only a bigger screen but a front facing the camera as well. The device boasts software and hardware updates.

What sets the Fire Tablet apart from the rest? It is available in 4 colors (Red, Blue, Yellow & Black). It offers up to 12 hours of battery life, an eight-inch HD display and 1.5GB of RAM. Your device also comes with either 16 or 32 GB of storage depending on the amount chosen. You also have the option to increase your memory size too, at most, 256 GB. The HD tablet also offers Amazon-specific features like On Deck, ASAP, X-Ray Free Time Controls, For You and Blue Shade.

Your Fire HD Tablet isn't alone. It joins a family of great devices. These devices include the Fire HD 7 and the Fire HD 10. Don't forget, with your device you also get a free month of Prime. This allows users to take advantage of all of the things your Fire HD Tablet can offer and get a jump start on using your Prime Membership.

This book will provide you with all of the information needed in order to not only use the basic functionalities but to get the most out of your Amazon experience. If this is your first device with Amazon, I'm sure it will not be your last. This guide will work with you from the setup onward. It will add you in customizing your device, troubleshooting your devices and using some features you may not even know existed. Grab your device and let's engage on a journey through your Amazon HD Device.

1 Chapter – Unboxing & Getting Started With Your Fire HD Device

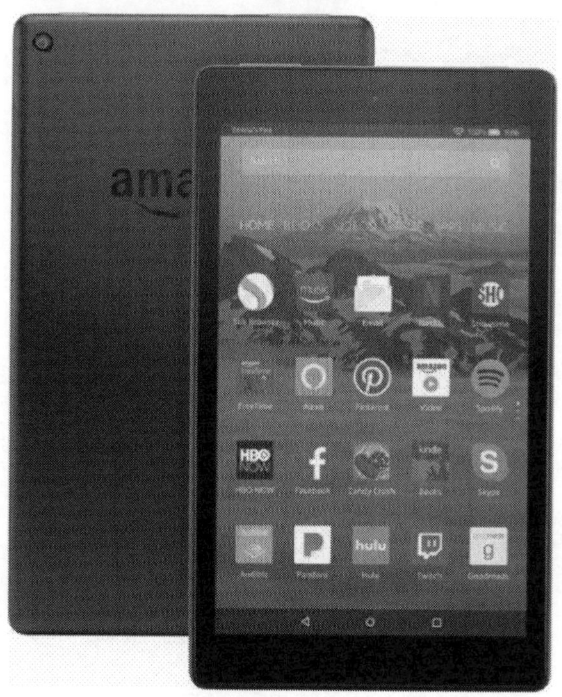

Device Specifications

Your Amazon Fire HD 8 is an 8-inch-high definition touchscreen device. It has a 12800 x 800 resolution. The dimensions for the device are 8.4" x 5.0" x 0.4". It possesses a 1.3 GHz quad-core processor and is equipped with 1.5 GB of RAM.

Your Fire HD device is also equipped with 16 or 32 GB of expandable storage. You may expand your memory up to 256 GB.

What's in the Box?

Congratulations on your new Amazon Fire HD 8 tablet. If you haven't opened your box yet this section will give you a sneak peek into what to expect. In your box, you can find the following:

Fire HD Tablet

USB 2.0 Cable

5W power adapter

Quick Start Guide

Once you pull your device from the box you will notice a few things in terms of its physical features.

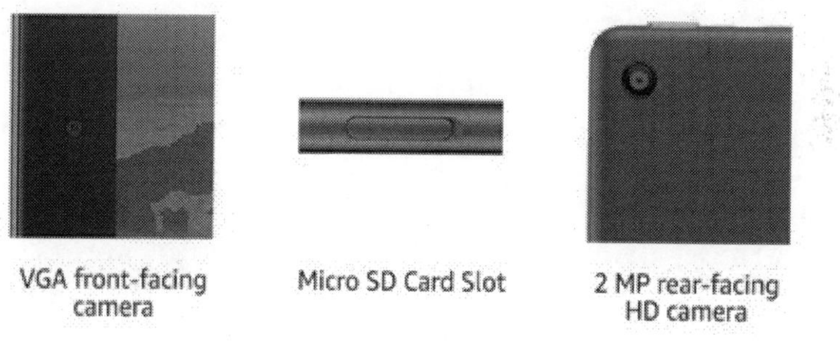

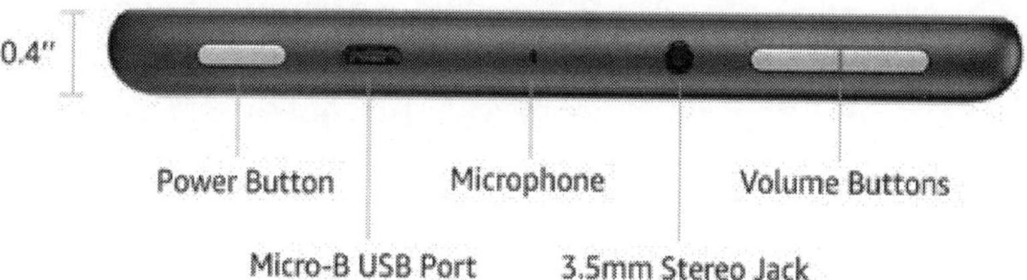

How to Power on Your Device

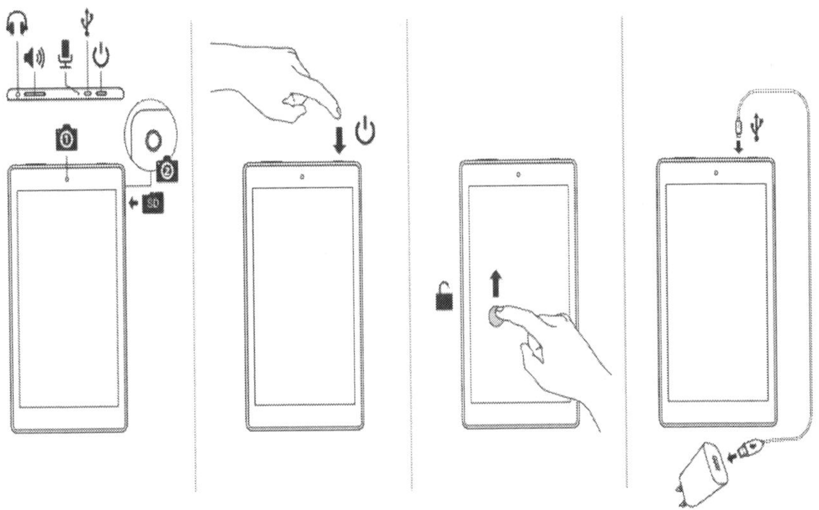

The very top of your device you will find a host of ports and controls. As you can see in the image above, these (left → right) are your headphone jack, volume controls, speaker, USB port and power button. On the front of your device, you will find a front-facing camera, the rear-facing camera on the backside and on the side an expandable memory card slot.

Your device does not come with a completely dead battery, to get started with your device simply press the power button until the screen is triggered. Your device will adjust its display to the direction which it is being held, landscape or portrait. When your device is turned on and finished loading you will see a splash screen like the one shown below. You will need to select your desired language and press the continue button which will be in the bottom right-hand corner of your screen.

Once you have chosen the correct language for your device, you can now choose to connect the WI-FI to your home network. This is required in order to finish the setup of your new Fire HD Device. The Fire HD is capable of detecting any close-range Wi-Fi networks, as well as, any Wi-Fi hotspots. Enabling a wireless network allows you to begin searching the web and downloading the applications. Select the name of your wireless network which you would like to connect to. Once you have selected the name to enter your password information and choose Connect. If it has connected properly you should receive a notification stating that the network has been connected. Depending on when your item was purchased you may be prompted to download an Amazon update. Allow your device to update before continuing setup.

Connecting Wi-Fi on Your Device After Initial Setup

If you skipped the setup of your Wi-Fi Network during your initial setup, never fear it can be accessed at any time. After you have finished setup your device and would like to connect a network, simply navigate to your quick settings panel. Follow the steps below to fully set up your internet connection.

Pull downward on the notification panel and from the quick settings select Swipe select Wi-Fi.

You will need to toggle the switch to the onward position to enable your Wi-Fi.

Once you have turned the Wi-Fi on you will see a listing of Networks which you may connect to. Choose the desired network. If the lock icon appears next to an item a password will be needed. Although some networks may require a password in order to connect, others may not.

If you have chosen a network with a lock enter your password and select connect.

Registering Your Amazon Device

Once your device has finished updating you will now need to associate your device with your Amazon account. If you purchased this item using your Amazon account it will come already associated with that account. If this is the account you would like to use, you will need to confirm it is the correct account and enter the password. If you did not purchase your item from Amazon you will see the screen below.

Simply log in or create an Amazon account to use with the device.

In order to utilize you Fire device to its fullest potential, this includes purchasing music or apps, your device must be registered to Amazon account.

If you are looking to use your device in order to buy content or have content wirelessly delivered to you, you will need to associate your device with a valid Amazon Account.

If you chose to forego the set-up of an Amazon account when starting your device, the following steps may be used in order to go back through the process:

On the top of your screen swipe downward on the quick settings menu. From the menu, listing chooses the Settings option.

Once you are within the settings menu choose My Account and then select the register option.

After you have chosen to register the device you will have 2 options. These options will include the following:

If you already have an Amazon account you will simply need to enter your login credentials. You even have the option to reset your password if you have forgotten

If you are void of an Amazon Account, you have the option to register for one. In order to do so simply select 'Start Here' and follow the instructions provided by the device.

After you have logged in or confirmed your account. You will potentially be prompted to restore a backup from another device.

The screen will look as shown below:

You may choose to tap Restore or Do Not Restore.

The next step in setting up your device will be altering the Time zone settings. Along with this option, you will have the option to do the following:

Enable your location services

Save your Wi-Fi password to Amazon

AutoSave your Photos & Videos

Backup & Restore your device

Select Continue in order to continue your set up of the Fire device. This will take you to a screen where you will be prompted to connect your social media accounts to your device. This would include Twitter, Facebook, and GoodReads. To continue with your setup tap, Get Started Now. You will be presented with a series of promotional options and trial memberships in order to get acquainted with some of Amazon's most popular item.

2 Chapter – Using Your Fire HD Device

Using Your Quick Settings

Your quick settings menu includes the following:

Brightness – This allows the user to adjust the rightness on the screen. Simply drag the slider in order to do so.

Wi-Fi – This area allows for the setup and editing of any connectivity. Your Wi-Fi can be turned on or off as needed.

Airplane Mode – Use this mode when you are flying.

Blue Shade – This mode is ideal for night time reading, adding a slight hue to the screen

Do Not Disturb – This mode prevents any notifications from disturbing the user.

Camera – This simply launches the camera.

Help – This area provides a guide to the user for the most common issues they would be experiencing.

Auto-Rotate – This allows your device to rotate its screen

orientation as it is turned.

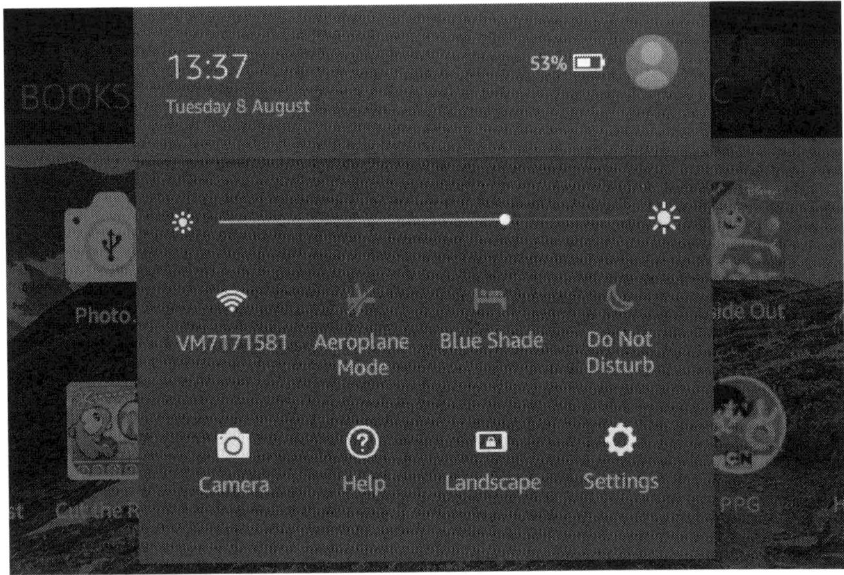

The Options Bar

The options bar is shown on every screen of your device. A sample of this is shown above. The options on this bar will vary based on the content type being displayed. However, the options shown above are the standard options for the bar. These base options include the following:

Home: This option will take you back to your home screen.

Back: This option will take you back to the previous screen of the device.

Menu: This option will allow you to view additional options, which are not shown.

Search: This will allow you to search the content of the content library you are currently in.

The arrow you see above is hidden when apps are running. In order to expand, you must simply swipe up on the arrow, this will reveal the navigation bar.

Using the Navigation Bar

The navigation bar can be shown from any and every screen. Even in full-screen mode, your navigation bar can be activated. In order to activate the navigation bar in the middle of the screen or move your hand down from the upper portion of the screen.

Once activated, you will find 3 buttons. These include the following items:

This will send you to your home screen or to the last content page that you visited.

This will take you to the previous page.

This is used to open your current list of running tasks. From here you have the ability to view, open or close any recent apps.

Alexa on Your Fire HD Tablet

Did you know that you can now utilize Alexa on your Fire HD tablet? Alexa now comes pre-installed with your very own virtual assistant, Alexa. Alexa is Amazon's leading lady in the smart assistant realm. Although more notably known for her presence on the Amazon Echo suite of devices, she is no longer a stranger to the tablet world. Although you may have an Echo Dot or general Echo device using Alexa on your Fire device will provide a different experience.

In order to get started with Alexa, hold down your Home button. You will eventually see a blue line on your screen which means Alexa has been activated successfully. She is now ready for her first command.

It is important to note that if your device is in sleep mode or if the lock screen is active, Alexa cannot be awakened. However, one amazing feature about Alexa on your tablet is that it can provide visuals to go with your requests, much like the Echo Show. On-screen features can be dismissed by simply tapping outside of the box

If Alexa is not your style, no worries, simply turn her off. This can be done from within the settings menu of the device. Once inside of the settings navigate to Device Options and choose Alexa's toggle button. If there are any parental controls set up on the device, Alexa will automatically be turned off. She cannot work in conjunction with any child-centered profiles.

Securing Your Fire HD Device

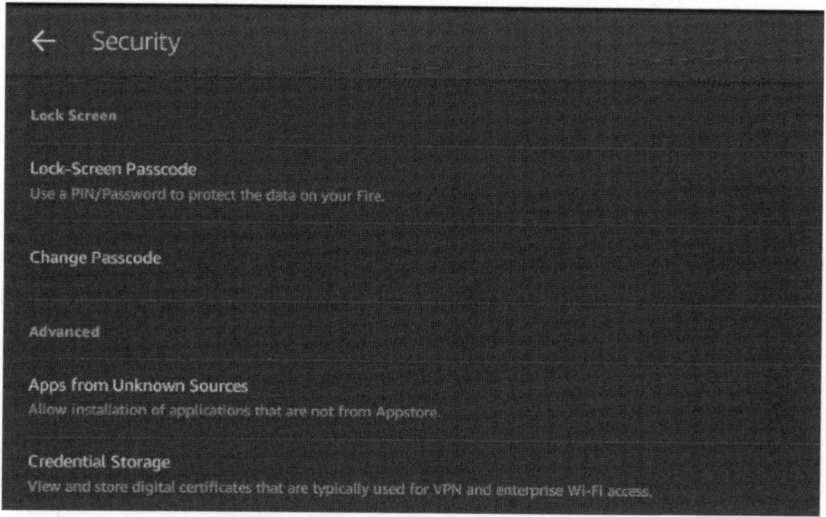

How to Add a Pin to Your Device

Adding a pin to your device is a great way to secure unwanted users from having access to your device. On your Fire HD 8 device, patterns or pins can be created to provide an added level of security. Whenever your device is awakened from sleep mode it will show. This screen will include the time, date and any unseen notifications. It will also display whatever profiles are available for your device. This includes the ability to switch between household accounts.

In order to implement a lock screen on your device follow the instructions below:

Swipe downward on your screen in order to see the notification tray and select Settings.

While in the settings area tap Security.

You will see the Lock Screen Passcode title with a toggle next to it. Toggle the setting to on.

In order to create a numerical passcode, tap PIN. If you are looking to create something alphanumerical, choose the password. A more complex password will make it harder for someone to guess your passwords.

Child Protectants: Monitoring Your Child's Activity

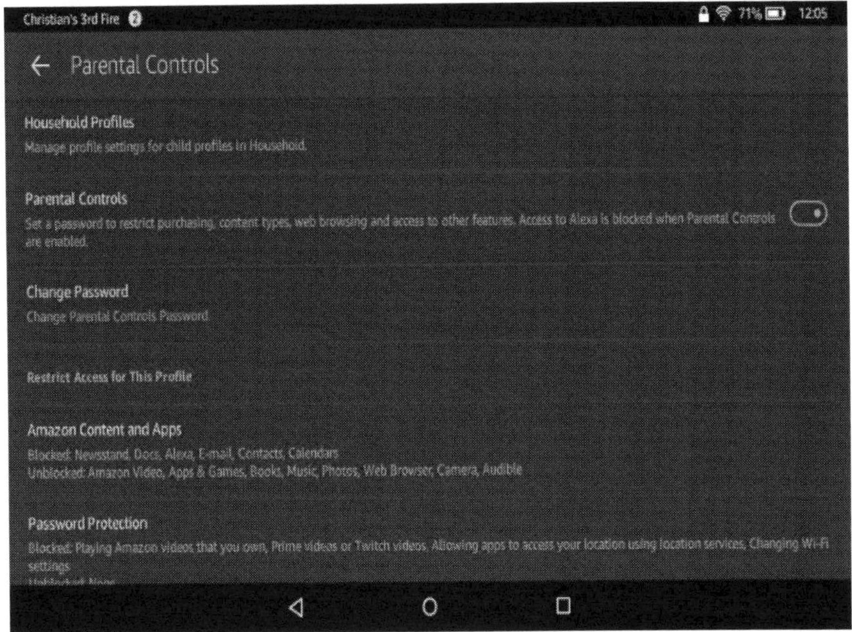

If you have purchased this device for a child and you are interested in setting up parental controls, the Activity Center will be your friend. This is a great way to see exactly what it is your child is doing on the tablet. It will even provide you with the amount of time spent utilizing the device.

For the activity center to begin collecting information related to your child's usage you must first follow the instructions below in order to begin.

While inside of the Settings area, select the Parental Controls section. In order to gain access, you must enter the password which you have set up for the device.

Select the option which reads **Monitor This Profile**.

Once logged in you will see the following icon for all devices which you are checking, This icon will be located on the top of the device's screen.

Once clicked, this area will give information on the time spent performing activities, listening to music and a variety of other information. You can also look at what sites were visited by your child as well as what apps are being used.

Sharing Content Across a Family

With Household profiles, Amazon profiles a good way for users to share content amongst each other. This is done with the Family Library and shared content section. The Household application allows users to share content with the cloud. Each user has the ability to filter what they would like with to share with others connected to the household.

In order to begin sharing content, you will need authorization from all Household parties. It is also important to remember that payment methods from all household accounts can be shared as well. However, when it is deleted from Household it is deleted from all accounts and devices connected to the household account.

To begin setting up your Family Library follow the instructions below:

Add an account to your Amazon Household

From the settings choose Profiles & Family Library.

Select the Account which you would like to create a Family Library with. You then need to choose Enable Sharing.

In order to share and confirm your payment selection, select continue.

Lastly, you will need to choose the types which you would like to share with others. Other associated users will need to follow these same instructions.

Please note that once you select a content type all will be shared with others in the Household collection. This includes all current and future purchases.

Receiving Notifications on Your Fire HD

If you are looking for a way to mute or unmute any notifications from your device, the quick settings area will be your best friend. Although your device will make a sound when plugged in for charging all notifications can be toggled on or off.

If you are looking to view current notifications simply swipe down from the top of your screen in order to reveal your notifications tray. To interact with or open a notification simply tap the item or select 'dismiss all' to clear the tray. You may also swipe specific items left or right in order to get rid of them. This interaction can also be carried out from the lock screen as well. Altering the notifications from your lock screen can also be turned off from within your settings. You will need to select "When the device is locked" and select your preferences for notifications. Tapping does not disturb will also mute all of your notifications until it is changed.

In order to alter specific notifications, select an application from the listing of applications in order to allow or disallow a notification to appear in the tray. You can also edit the default notification sound from the Sound & Notification settings.

Managing Your Device Storage

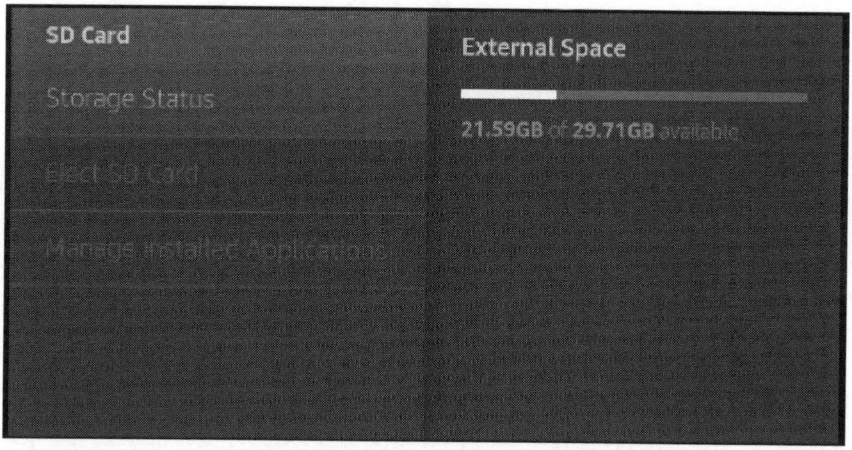

Your device storage is an important piece of usage for your Fire HD device. Managing your storage is essential to being able to continue to save and use your device. In doing so, there are a variety of changes which can be made on your device in order to optimize storage. Managing these preferences is simple. Use the instructions below in order to manage and update your preferences.

In order to begin, swipe downward on the device from the notification tray and choose the Settings options. From within the settings choose Storage, in order to edit your storage settings.

Under the SD Card settings, you can choose which items will be saved to your SD card. This can be altered using the switches for each category. By design, categories are automatically downloaded by the micro SD.

Choose the content category which will allow you to alter where information in that category is saved.

You can also move content to and from your SD card. This is an easy process and can be done using the method below.

How to Move Applications to Your Memory Card

Swipe downward and select the Settings. You will then need to select App & Games.

Choose Manage All Applications and choose the application in which you would like to move.

The steps utilize the following steps: **Settings → Storage → Move Apps to SD Card**.

How to Move Music to Your SD Card

In order to move music from your device, in order to free up space on your device, follow the steps listed below:

From your main screen select the Music option.

Choose the menu option and select settings.

Once you have got into the music settings, choose the option to Transfer All Offline Music. Then you will need to select Transfer All to SD Card.

To move other media types downloaded from an Amazon source to your microSD card, you should first remove them from your HD Fire device. Once they have been deleted they can be re-downloaded after the SD card has been inserted into the device.

Inserting & Removing Your Micro SD

Your Micro SD card gives you the ability to store a vast amount of information. This may be pictures, videos or documents. This adds a whole new dimension to the use of the Fire HD Tablet.

In order to insert and remove your SD card, follow the

instructions below:

Start by holding your device vertically. Your camera should be positioned at the utmost middle of the device. If your camera is at the bottom you are holding it wrong. The SD card slot is located on the upper right side of the Fire HD device.

In order to insert or remove, you need to open the card cover. Position your device in order to make the slot easier to see. Push your new SD card into the slot, when it is in you will feel it lock. The images below will guide you through this process.

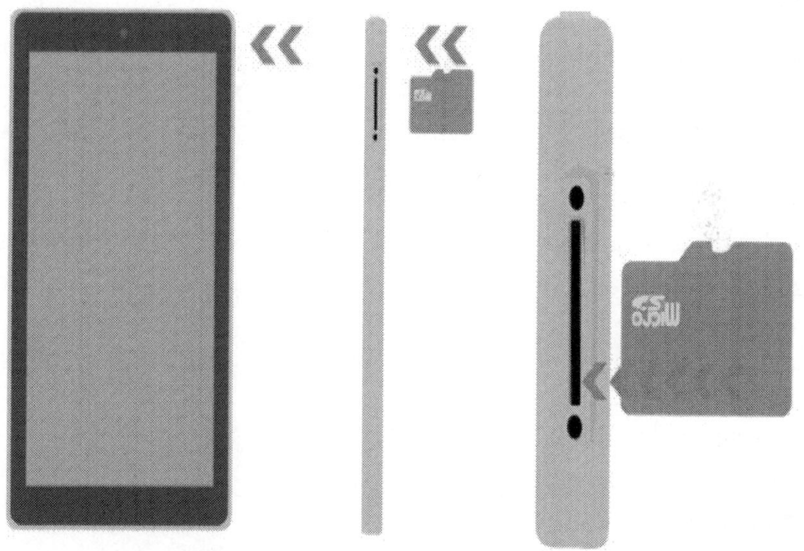

Removing the SD card operates in the same fashion as an insertion with only a few extra steps.

Before removing the card, you must eject it from the HD device. To do so, Swipe downward on the notifications tray from the highest point on your screen and press settings.

Once in the 'Settings' select the "Safely remove SD Card".

Start by holding your device vertically. Your camera should be positioned at the top center of the device. If your camera is at the bottom you are holding it wrong. The SD card will be on the upper right-hand side of your device.

Rather than inserting the card, press down on the card to unseat it. From there you should be able to pull the card from the device.

3 Chapter – Media on Your Fire HD Device

Being that the Kindle Fire is a media device it would only be right that the Fire Tablet is used as an entertainment device. With this device, you can read, watch and even listen from a number of sources.

Finding & Downloading Games & Applications

Games and applications are essential to your media experience with your tablet. All Fire Tablets provide users with the option to search and download a multitude of games and various other content.

In order to complete any purchasing through the Amazon app store, you will need to have a payment method on file and set up within your one-click settings. When downloading a game or app, you are not required to have a card on file for free app purchases – this applies to U.S residents only. However, remember that some games or apps do offer in-app purchases. However, this can be toggled on or off.

Downloading & Searching Games & Apps

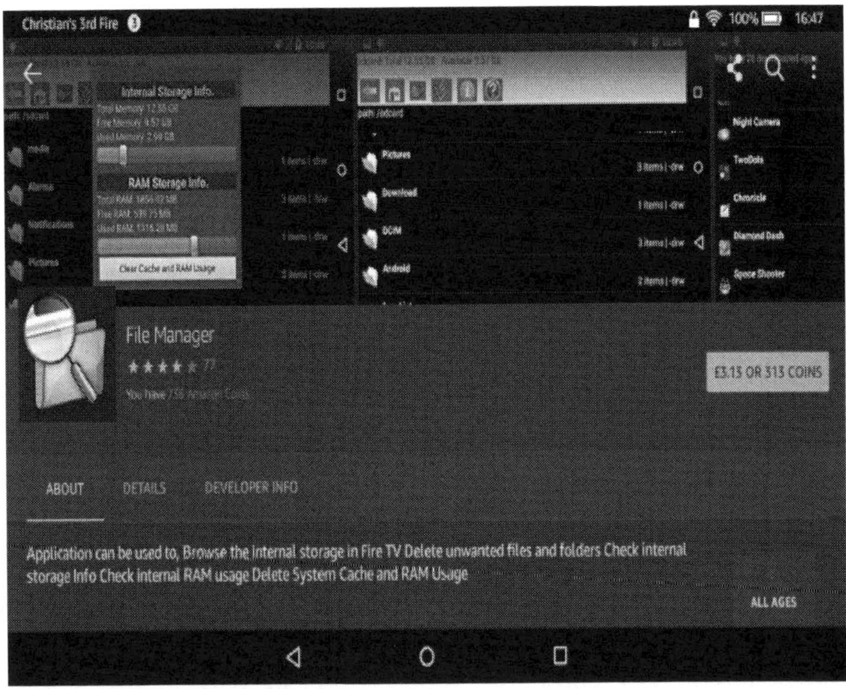

In order to begin downloading items to your device, from your home screen tap on Apps and navigate to the Store.

Once inside of the store, locate the app or game which you are searching for.

If you already know the name of the item, tap the search icon, the magnifying glass, in the bottom right corner in order to begin the search for the device.

To limit your search results, filter the options. This can be done by simply selecting the filter icon and sorting or choosing specific details about the product.

Once on the detailed page of the application, you will see a multitude of information. This will include any pricing. The price will also serve as your download button. If you're buying something that requires a money purchase, 1 click payment will need to be enabled in order to continue.

Once your download has completed tap the icon on the newly downloaded application in order to open it. Your item will be updated automatically going forward. Manual updates will need to be done by you, the user on the app store if needed.

It is important to note that Amazon coins can also be used to purchase applications and games.

Videos on Your Fire HD

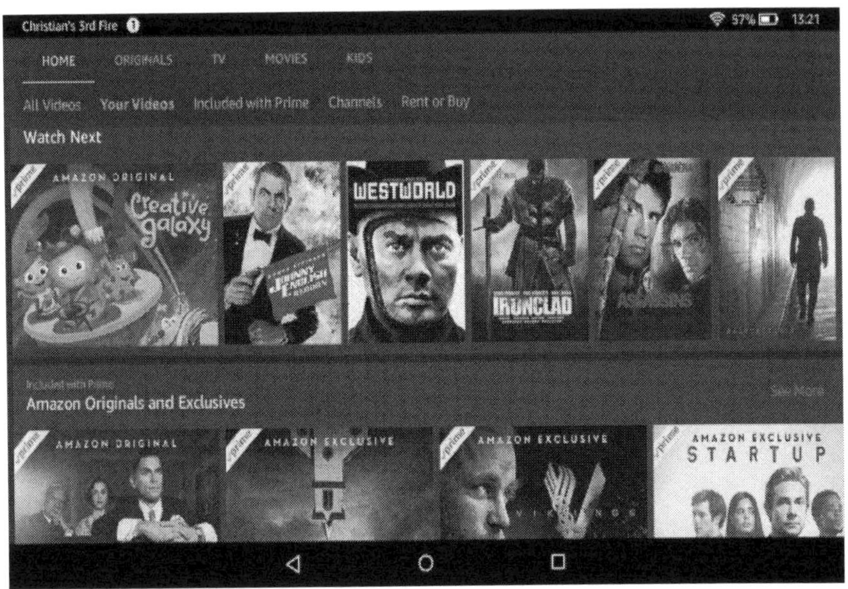

If didn't know, Amazon Video can be used on the Fire HD tablet. Your tablet not only gives you the ability to play downloaded material but also stream a variety of content as a well from Amazon and Netflix. The video capabilities of your tablet are also particularly helpful when you have an Amazon Prime membership.

With a Prime membership, you can rent or purchase videos directly from your tablet. However, when renting videos, your items are only eligible for a certain length of time while purchased videos can be watched whenever you feel the urge.

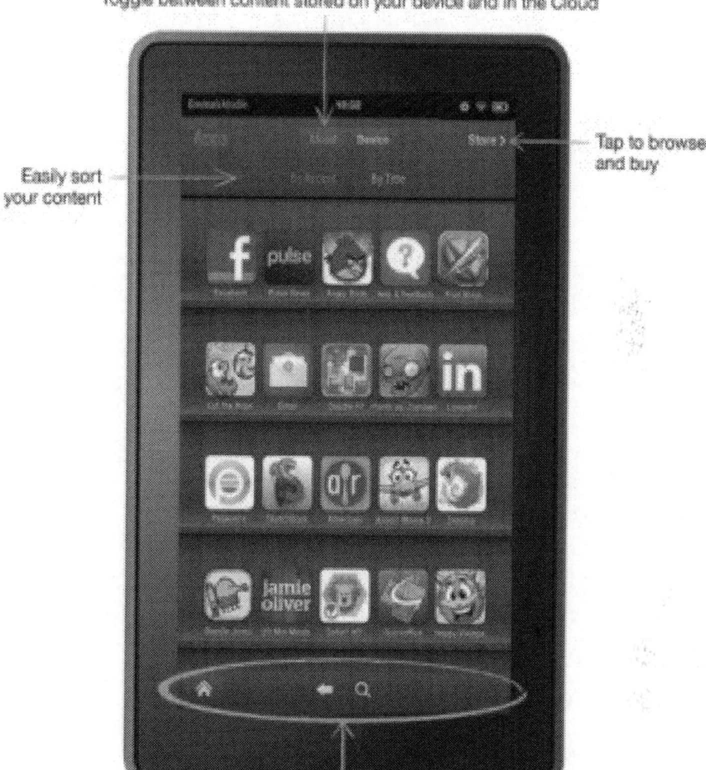
Toggle between content stored on your device and in the Cloud
Tap to browse and buy
Easily sort your content
The Options bar contains icons such as Home, Back, and Search

Your device can also handle content which has been transferred to your device from a computer. In order to get your full listing of videos available select Video from the category bar on the top of your screen.

From the Video Section and tap Store in order to rent or buy any video content. In order to complete a purchase, 1 click payment settings must be enabled in order to be automatically charged for your items.

As you know, Amazon offers a wide variety of subscriptions

services, products, and items for you to purchase directly from Amazon or through a variety of third-party vendors. This makes purchasing items on your Fire HD device as simple as 123. This also includes music, magazines and so much more. Please note that anything purchased through Amazon will appear on your device in the designated area.

Music on Your Fire HD Device

Your Fire HD device can also serve as a hub for all of your music needs. Any music which has been downloaded from Amazon will appear in your personal library. Any other downloaded materials can also be found within your Music Library.

Adding, Navigating & Deleting Music from Your Device

Adding music to your Amazon Library is simple. To add music to your Amazon Music Library simply tap browse. Find the music which you are looking to add and tap the Add button for songs. If you are attempting to add an album hit the 'Add album to the library' button or for playlists, 'add playlists to library'.

The 'more options' icon will be used for a majority of your music related changes. This includes:

Downloading Music: From the more options menu select Download

Deleting or removing music from a device

Deleting or removing music from the cloud

Create or alter playlists

It is important to remember that if an item has been removed from your library and is a paid item, it will need to be bought again from the Music Store.

How to Begin Reading on Your Tablet

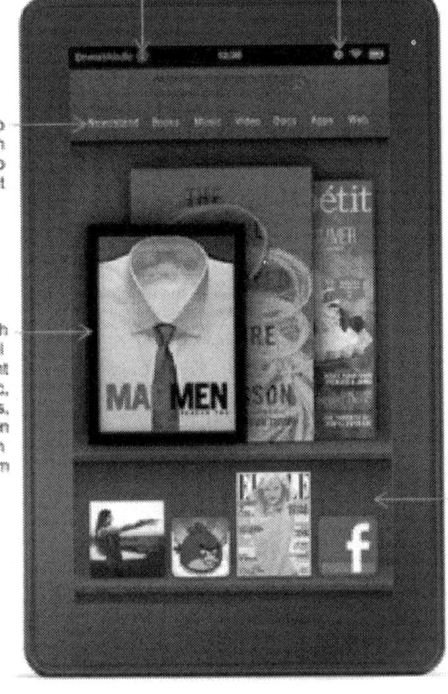
Tap Notifications to read messages from the system or apps
Tap Quick Settings to adjust volume or brightness, manage Wi-Fi, and more
Tap here to switch between libraries or to shop for content
Swipe through the Carousel to view recent books, music, videos, websites, and apps, then tap to open an item
Pin your favorite content here by tapping and holding an item in the Carousel

Amazon is known for the quality of their readers and the Kindle Fire is no different.

Syncing Your Progress

It is always assumed that users have multiple devices therefore syncing progress is essential. The Fire HD device gives users the ability to sync across multiple devices which utilize the Kindle Application.

This can even be done while reading or before exiting your reading session. In order to provide a full sync with your account, tap the middle of the screen in order to display the menu bar. You will see an icon in the top left corner of the menu. Select this and select sync. This will bring all your devices up to date.

Going Back to Your Location of a Book

When navigating back to the location in a Kindle book, this location is specific to your Kindle format and not the page numbers within the physical copy of the book. Kindle does, however, give you the ability to alter this within your settings. Page numbers on your device, however, do correlate to the books print edition.

Kindle items also include the Time to Read feature. This is what is used in order to calculate your reading time. This lets you know how much time is left before you finish your book or even your chapter. The speed information does not sync and is specific to the device you are using.

Your Reading Progress

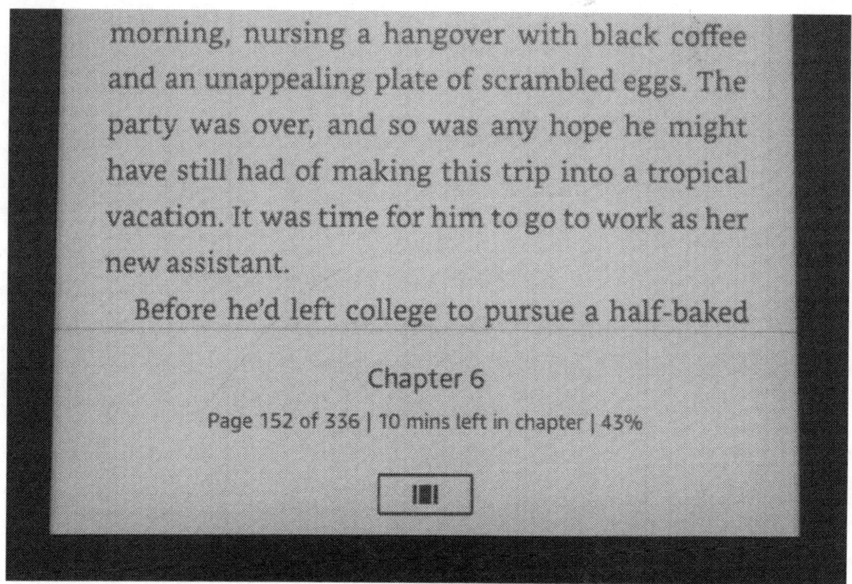

morning, nursing a hangover with black coffee
and an unappealing plate of scrambled eggs. The
party was over, and so was any hope he might
have still had of making this trip into a tropical
vacation. It was time for him to go to work as her
new assistant.
Before he'd left college to pursue a half-baked
Chapter 6
Page 152 of 336 | 10 mins left in chapter | 43%

If you are ever interested in knowing your specific progress for a book, tap the center of your screen while reading. This will provide you with a progress bar as well as show the page flip functionality.

Your progress is provided to users as a percentage of the progress bar. To navigate to different sections of the book simply swipe left or right. You may also use Back to in order to jump back to a specific page or section.

Other key performance indicators include the following:

Navigating to the next or earlier page: Use this feature by selecting the right side of the screen for next and the left side of the previous page.

Navigate to a specific page: From the top left menu select 'Go' and enter the page number you would like to go to.

Navigate to a specific Chapter or section: To jump to a specific chapter or heading simply scroll up or down until you see the section you are searching for. Tap the heading to be taken to the first page of that section.

Customizing Your Reading Experience

Customization is no stranger to the Fire HD device, this includes within the realm of reading various content. Many people have changing preferences for font size, margin sizing, etc. The Fire HD tablet provides users the ability to customize their experience. There are several items that can be changed in order to enhance the reading experience. This includes:

Fonts

Line spacing

Margins,

Background color

If you wish to alter any of these features simply tap the center of your screen in order to display the reading toolbar. You will then notice an Aa, this can be used to edit properties of your book.

To change the font size, utilize the + or the – in order to increase or decrease the font sizes. Tap until your desired size is reached.

Setting Line Spacing & Margins

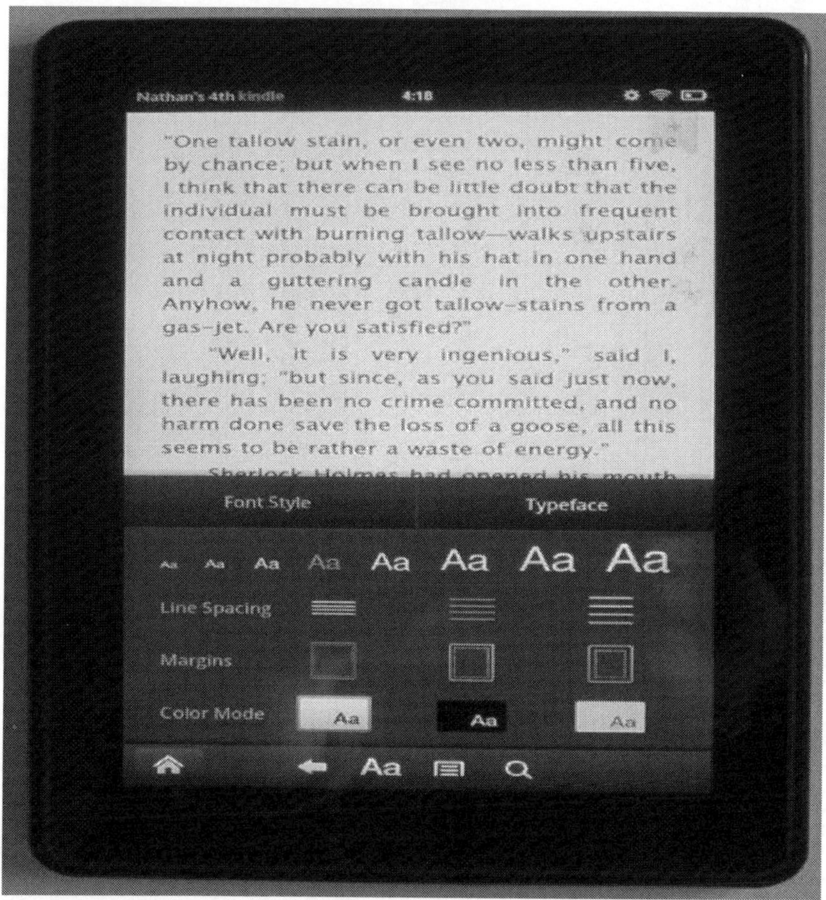

The line spacing, margins, and color are also able to be changed from within the font settings area.

When changing the color, the user can select the desired color scheme for the background. There are 3 options for colors. These include White, green, sepia or black.

To change margins, simply choose narrow, wide or normal. There are currently the only 3 size options available. This will change the look of space on the left or right side of the page.

Last but not least, line spacing can be changed by choosing the same limited options as the margins. This includes narrow, wide or normal.

Listening & Reading Simultaneously

If you are someone who enjoys the idea of following along as they read or while listening to audio books, Immersion reading gives you the ability to do just that. To utilize this feature, you will need to own the audiobook, as well as the Kindle book.

In order to begin using Immersion reading, utilize the steps outlined in this section.

If you already own the product which you are attempting to read, simply navigate to your library and search for your already owned items. Once you get to the detail page for the selected item, tap the add Narration button. It will be shown if the product is eligible for Immersion Reading. You will then be able to purchase the audiobook and download.

If you do not own any of the books which you would like to read using Immersion reading, go to the books library and swipe in from the left edge of the screen. From this area choose Immersion Reading. This will allow you to browse the titles which are able to use this feature and purchase the needed items. Only then will you will be able to activate Immersion Reading.

Once you have books which are eligible for immersion reading tap the headphone icon on your item and press play to hear the narration and see the highlighting within the text.

Read and listen at the same time

with Immersion Reading

Got a Kindle Fire HD? If so, you can also read and listen **Simultaneously** with real-time highlighting. It's called Immersion Reading and that's what it does: Immerse you in a story by narrating and highlighting the text as you read. It sparks an extra connection that boosts engagement, comprehension and retention, taking you deeper into the book.

Questions? Visit the FAQ page or call our Customer Care team anytime at 1-888-283-5051.

Available on Kindle Fire HD, Kindle Fire HDX, and Kindle Fire HDX 8.9"

4 Chapter – Advance Features of Your HD Fire

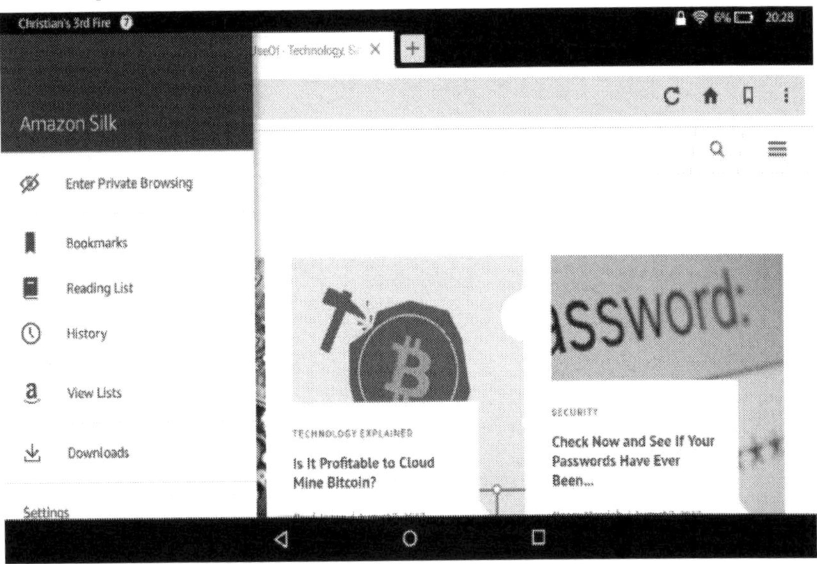

SILK Browser

If you didn't know about the SILK browser, this is Amazon's native browser. It is intended to create a more responsive experience when browsing via a mobile device. When this application is opened for the first time you will by default see the SILK homepage. You will by default see your most visited pages listed on the homepage, much like the Google homepage on Chrome. This will appear each time you open a new tab.

There are a variety of different feature available using the SILK browser, these include but are not limited to the following:

Navigating the web – This is the top feature of this application, being that it is a web browser. The browser will also provide users with suggestions based on your default search engine selected.

Page scrolling – Page scrolling is done simply by moving your finger up and down the page which you are viewing.

Reading View – Did you know SILK has a specific mode just for reading. Use the book icon in order to enhance your page for reading. This removes most graphics, advertisements or links from the page.

Enhanced features – Use the ⋮ icon in order to gain access to enhanced browser features. These features include

Entering and exiting private browsing.

Finding specific items on the page you are viewing. Simply select Find on Page.

Save items to your reading list – this feature allows the user to read items later in an offline capacity.

Zooming in and out – Zooming into and out of a web page is a very easy but needed feature. In order to zoom simply pinch two fingers together and un-pinch in order to zoom out.

Adding & Editing bookmarks

Printing – In SILK items can be printed traditionally or items can also be exported and saved as PDFs instead of printing.

Sharing – Sharing can be done via email or via various social media outlets.

Requesting of Mobile/Desktop Site – This can be used in order to see a generally desktop site in mobile version or switch the mobile version back to desktop version.

Mayday – Get the Help You Really Need ON Your Fire Tablet

You may be wondering what Mayday is and how it can help you. Don't worry, you aren't alone. Mayday is a toll which is available on all Fire Devices through the Quick Settings menu. This program allows users to communicate with an Amazon advisor from their devices. This advisor has the ability to walk users through specific features and even annotate on your device's screen. They can also aid you can tell you how to accomplish specific tasks you are looking to perform.

This feature is available at any time, 24/7. The advisor can see your screen throughout your session in order to help you with any wrong moves you may be making. This is included, for now, on a handful of devices which include the Kindle Fire HDX, the Fire HDX 8.9 and all of the Fire Phones.

How do I use Mayday?

If you are one of the lucky users to get Mayday on your device, use the following instructions in order to take full advantage and gain access to extra help with your device.

From the top of your screen swipe down and select the Mayday icon. The icon will look like the one listed here.

Once you are inside of the Mayday area, select connect.

If this is something you are not interested in, this feature can be turned off. To disable this feature, navigate to your settings and select Mayday. Simply turn the feature off from here.

Making the Most of Your Amazon Fire HD Experience

How to Change Your Device Name: Changing your device name can be helping when connecting to outside sources or even just wanting something recognizable. In order to change this name, use the following navigation trail. ***Settings → Device → Options →Change Your Device Name***

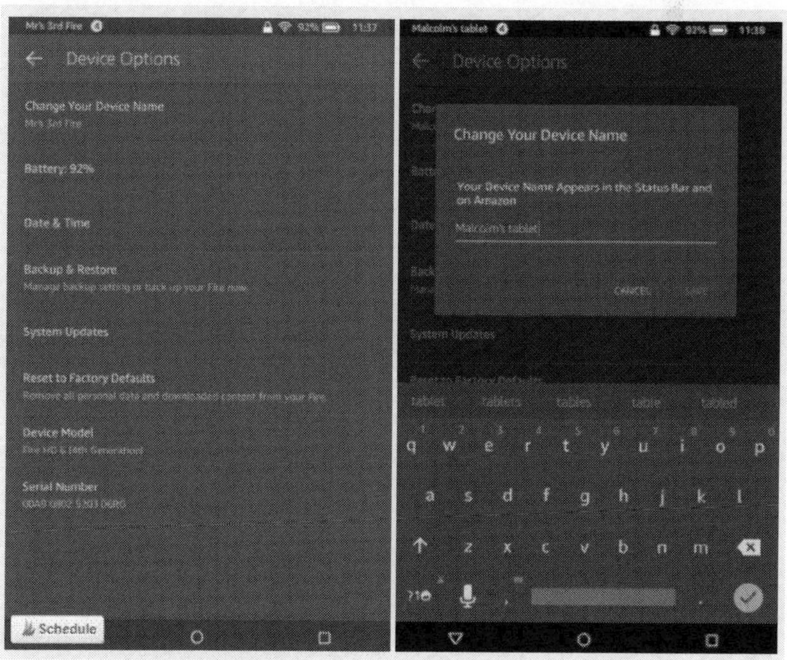

Customizing Your Device Wallpaper: You may be one of those people who leave the default background and you may not. Regardless of your preference, you have the option to change your wallpaper and add a little spice to your device. This can be done by navigating to the following trail. Navigate to Settings → Display → Wallpaper

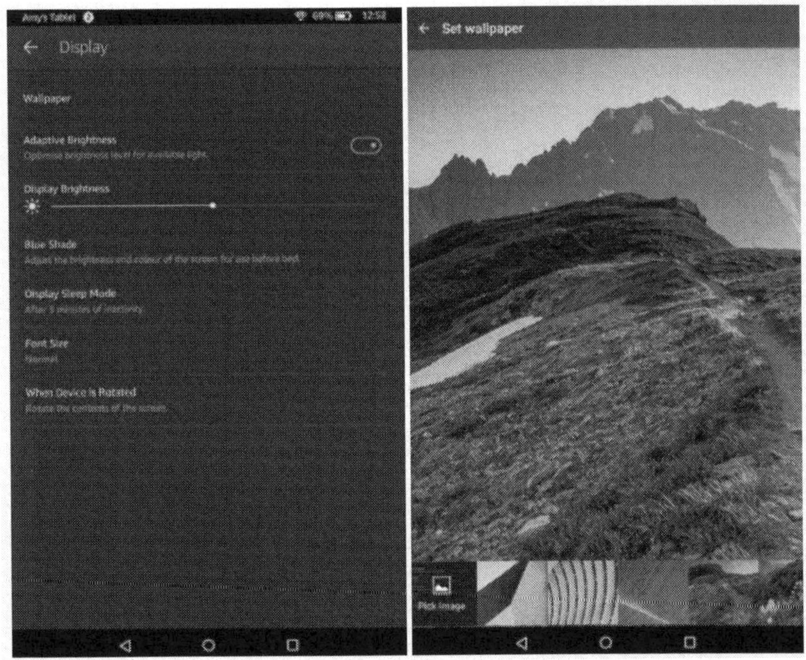

Screenshots are easy to take and always needed. To complete a screenshot on your device simply press the power and the down volume button.

5 Chapter – The Best Applications for Your Fire HD Tablet

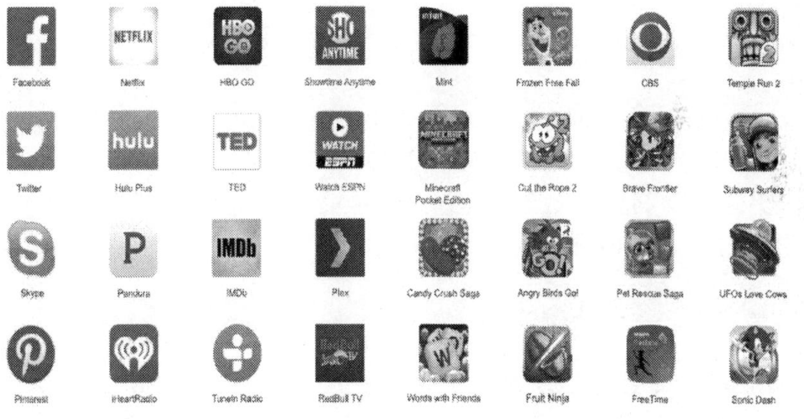

plus many more

Below you will find a list of applications which will aid you in using your Free HD Tablet. These are from a variety of different sources and are essential to providing you the best possible experience with your Fire HD Tablet. These applications are not based in order of importance but may all be used for different reasons.

These suggested applications work with your device and offer a function that is otherwise not provided or enhances your device's capabilities.

Skype

The Weather Channel

Evernote

Pocket

Netflix

Some applications are listed below which provide a range of added functionality and productivity to you while using your Kindle Fire HD. In the App Store if you look hard enough you will find something to fit any of your needs.

Minecraft: Pocket Edition

If you're looking for more items within the gaming realm, this is perfect for you. Although it comes in at a price point of 7 dollars, it is well worth the funds. It is said to be one of the most engaging mobile games of its time. It incorporates mind-blowing graphics as well as an interesting storyline.

Slacker Radio

Slacker Radio is another free radio application which can be used with the Kindle Fire HD. This is also a free application where a premium subscription can be purchased for 4.99 per month. Aside from music Slacker can also provide updates for things like weather and news.

Calorie Counter and Diet Tracker by MyFitnessPal

Are you looking to count calories and lead a healthier lifestyle? IS getting in shape part of your new year's resolution? This application is here to help. The MyFitnessPal application can be used to track your calorie intake as well as any exercise has done throughout the day. Information can be synced across all your applications using your common login. Many foods are already saved in the device and you can also save foods that you consume frequently. This app even has the ability to connect to smart trackers like Fitbit or Moto. This is a free application which is available to all users.

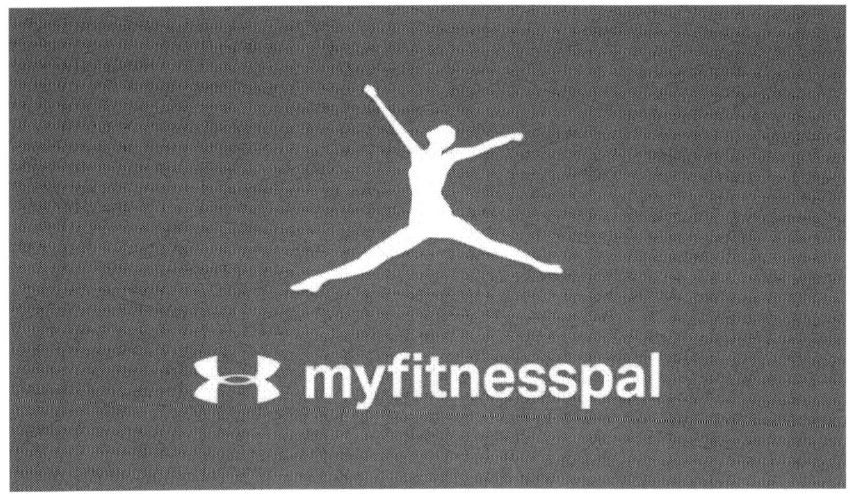

iHeartRadio

If you are a music lover and you are looking to stream radio programming and even radio stations this is the application for you. This app allows users to listen to some of their favorite radio stations. These can be music based or even talk radio, podcasts or comedy. Items can be streamed from wherever you have connected wireless network.

Spotify

If you are someone who is looking for flexibility when listening to music, playlists made by mood as well as curated playlists by genre, Spotify is the perfect application for you. Although it can be free, in order to gain customization privileges, you must pay for a premium membership. This comes at a price of 9.99 per month. With premium membership, you can also listen to any song on demand, no ads, as well as skip any undesirable song.

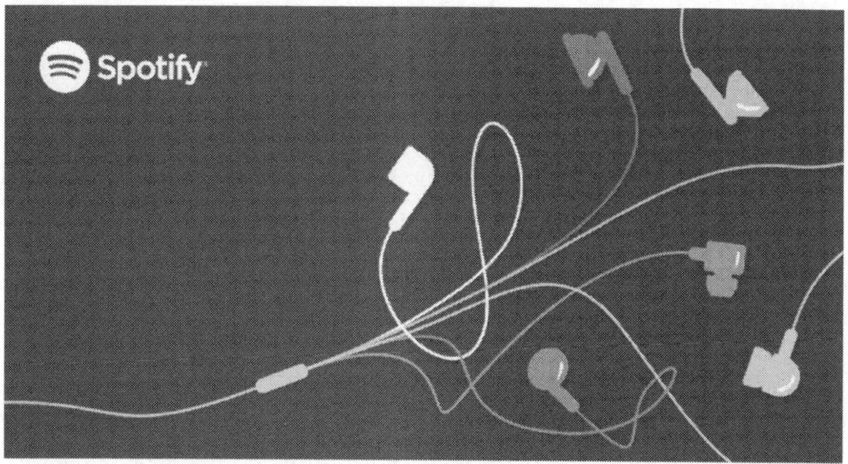

Easy Installer

Easy installer is a free application which allows users to sideload APKS onto their device. These aids users in downloading applications which are not from the Amazon App Store. This application aids the user in downloading the APK which it will need to run on the device.

Netflix

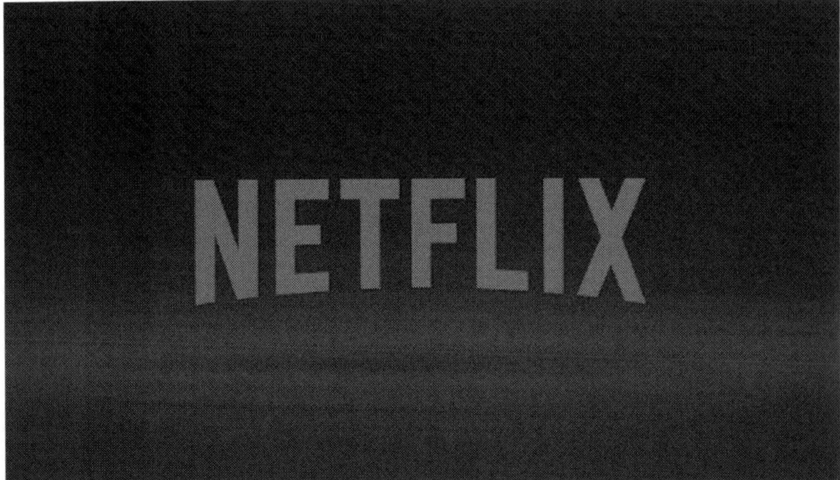

Netflix is a staple in all mobile devices. It allows users to watch a variety of television shows, Netflix originals, and movies. Watch popular favorites like Stranger things and Shameless in one subscription. Although the application is free to download, a subscription will cost you 7.99 a month. However, the price is small for the hours of entertainment you will enjoy. This is even an application which is compatible with the Chromecast, so stream away. On a long trip, never fear, connect your Wi-Fi and binge watch some of your favorite TV.

Office Suite Professional

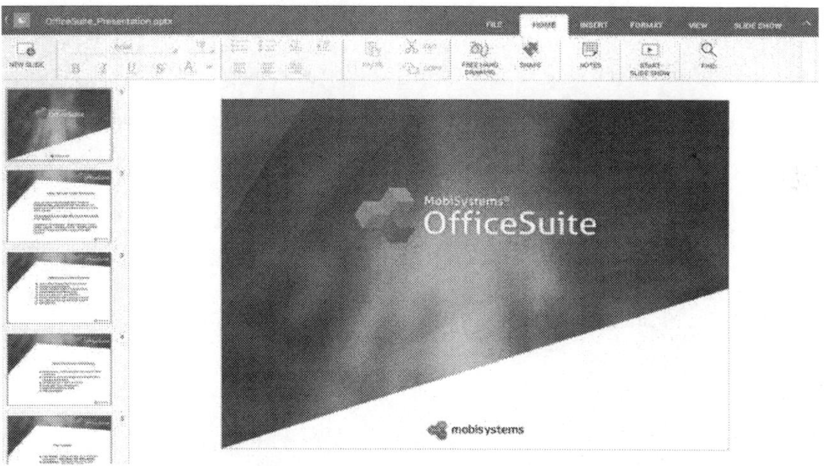

If you are an on the go professional, you can even use your device to edit documents and presentations on the fly. Keep your productivity at an all-time high with the Office Suite Professional Series. Along with presentations and documents, you also have the power to manipulate spreadsheets and so much more. Although this app is not free, for a one-time fee of 14.99 you can have it all.

OneNote

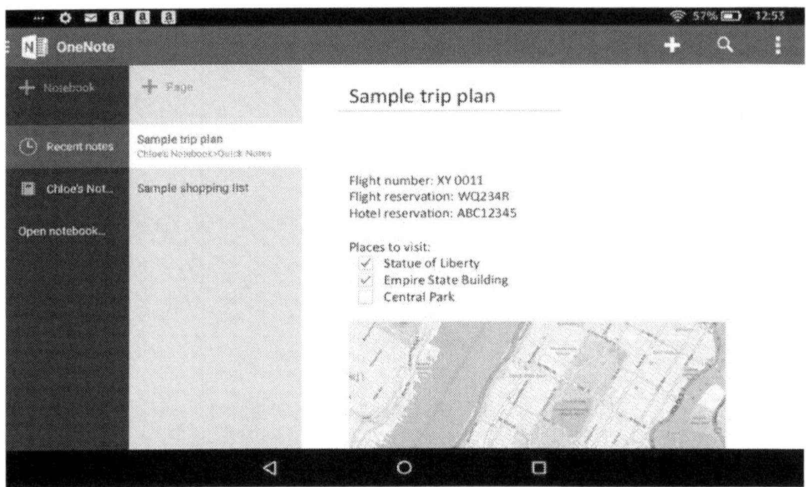

Another great application to increase your productivity is OneNote. This app allows you to take notes, create tasks lists or just brainstorm whenever needed. It also allows you the ability to record voice notes as well as add images to the pages of your virtual notebook. Sync your account across multiple devices by signing into a Microsoft account. You will never be without your notes again. This can be used for personal and professional purposes.

Food Network in the Kitchen

If you are someone who loves to cook and loves to try new things, this application is for you. The Food Network app is a free app which boasts a variety of recipes, tips, tricks and even instructional videos. The recipes are easy to read and provide plenty of information. This information may even include things like the recipe's difficulty level.

Pinterest

If you are always looking for new ideas and a way to share creations with others. Pinterest is the perfect application for you. This free application allows users to create visual bulletin boards where they can pin items of similar or varying categories. It can be used to find things like workouts, tutorials, and even recipes. Have a DIY project you want to share with the world? Use Pinterest.

Pocket

If you are looking to read more than just books on your Fire device, Pocket is a perfect addition to your app arsenal. This application gives users the ability to add websites to your current list of reading material even if there is no active Wi-Fi connection. It also allows to save your position on a page.

Goodreads on Kindle

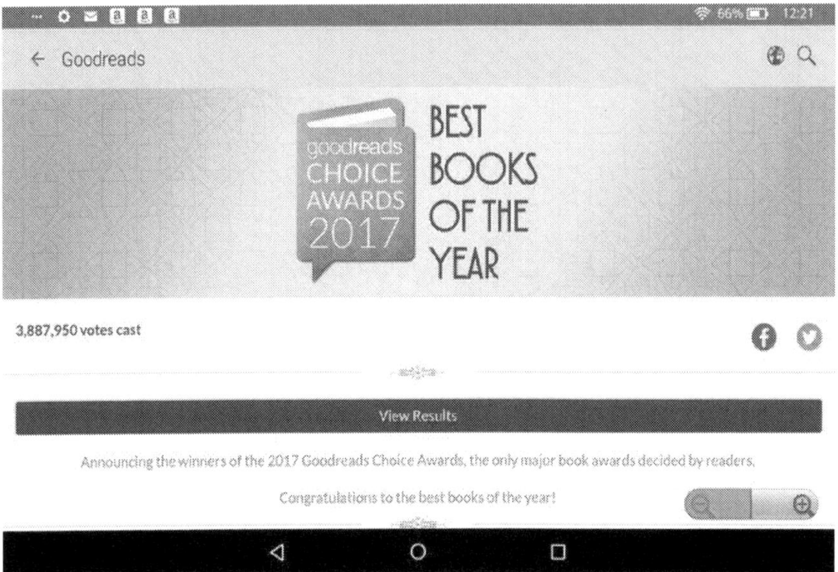

GoodReads is an app which Amazon stands by. Your Amazon account information is even the same login which will be used for GoodReads. This is a social media application which can be used to discuss and rate things you have read or are currently reading. It also gives users the ability to create lists of books they would like to read in the near future.

Remember the Milk

Remember the Milk is a very popular task management application. It helps you remember everything from the milk to the toilet paper. Create simple grocery lists or more complex lists of tasks for your personal life or even your job. The application is free, however, in order to get auto syncing the web version, you will need a pro subscription. You will also get notifications and alerts once you are a pro member. This will run you $25 per year.

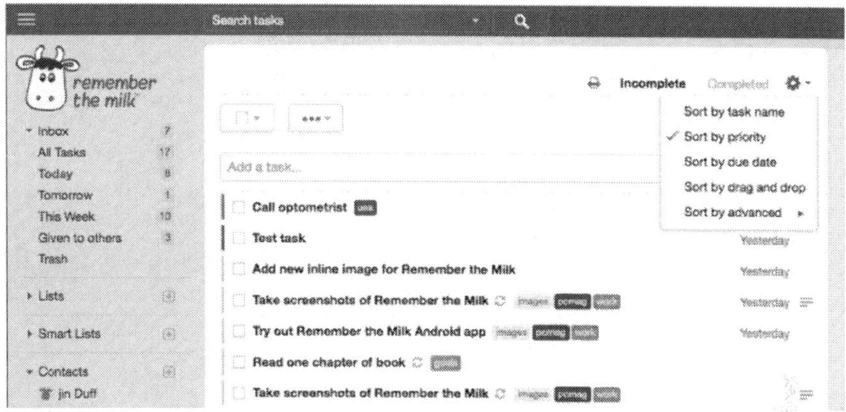

Plex

Plex is an application which is free to download and used as a media player system. This application allows for the playback of a variety of media items like photos, music, movies, and TV shows. With Plex, these items can be placed in a common repository and played across a variety of devices. Plex can be added to your personal computer or even your MAC book in order to add content. This content can then be played on your Kindle Fire HD. There are paid options for your Plex needs. This includes Plex Pass which comes with a variety of extra perks. This can be purchased for 5 dollars a month or 20 dollars a year.

Twitter

Although its popularity has waned, Twitter remains a favorite social network. It can be used to keep up with celebrity happenings or even keep up with friends and family. It can also be used as a second screen application. If you love to read short burst from random strangers or celebrities, this is for you.

AndroZip Pro File Manager (by AVG Labs)

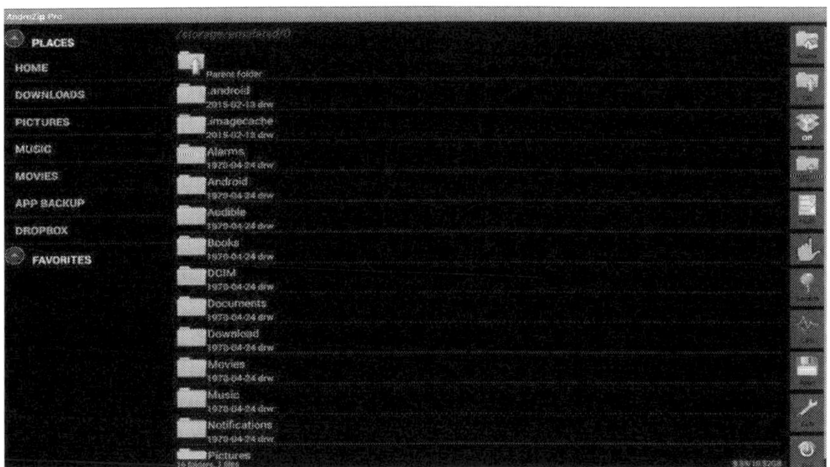

AndroZip Pro version is an application brought to the app store by AVG, a known anti-virus company. It allows users to delete, copy, search move and even organize all information which you choose to keep on your Fire HD Device. This also allows you to create and maintain folders the same way you would on a computer. It even comes fully equipped with drag and drop capability. Integration with Dropbox is also possible with this application.

Yelp

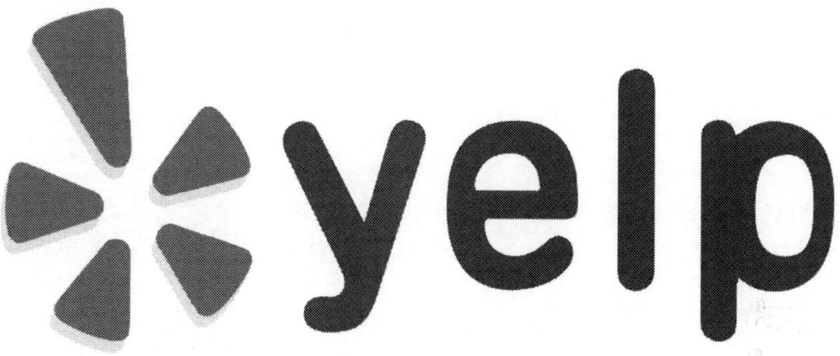

Do you love seeing customer reviews? Are you someone that wants to let others know about your horrible or wonderful experience? Do you look for ratings and reviews on restaurants and other attractions? If any of this describes you, Yelp is the perfect application. Yelp is an app all about business reviews from restaurants to doctors' offices. It also provides hours of operations. Take Yelp with you on your next trip in order to find the perfect restaurants and attractions.

LinkedIn Pulse

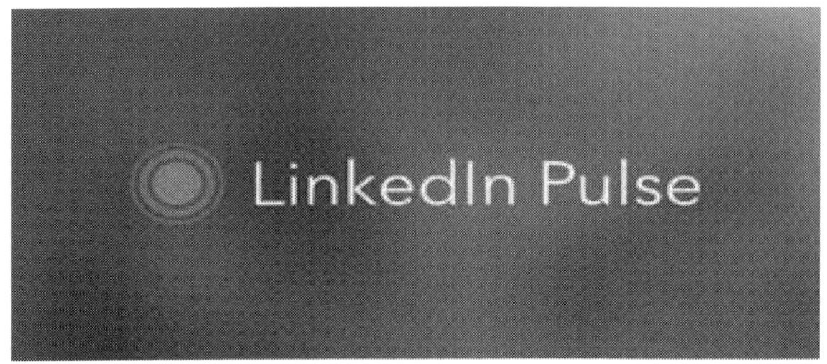

Are you a professional seeking a new job and hoping to make yourself marketable to others? LinkedIn is the Facebook of the professional world. Keep your resume updated and your professional contacts all within reach with this application. Advance your career in no time with this convenient and informational application.

Alarm Clock (by Apalon)

Never use a traditional alarm clock again with this free application. This app offers the ability to customize tones for your alarm, brighten or dim the device's screen and even provide weather reports to you in the AM. However, in the free version, there will be occasional ads. If you are looking to get rid of ads upgrade to the pro version for only 99 cents. Pro version also even lets you choose the music which will wake you up and put you back to sleep.

Bitdefender Antivirus Free

This is a free tablet which aids users in keeping their device safe from technological harm. Although the Fire HD is an Amazon device. It is still an Android device. This means that it is susceptible to Trojan horses, malware and a variety of malicious software. This application is a way to provide protection on an otherwise unprotected device. This adds a layer of protection and will also check when new apps are downloaded if they contain any malicious content. You also have the option to run periodic scans of your device to ensure that nothing slipped through the cracks and ensure that your device is running and operating as intended.

Amazon Underground

If you've never heard of Amazon Underground you are

missing out. This free application allows users to utilize and download a variety of usually premium and paid applications for FREE. This includes productivity applications, games and much more without paying a cent. This is already included on your Amazon Fire device and it's up to you to get started using it.

Comics (by comiXology)

If regular books aren't your style, you can even use your Kindle Fire to read comic books. The Comics application is perfect for the comic book lover in all of us. It not only allows you to read a variety of comics it also allows you to purchase them as well.

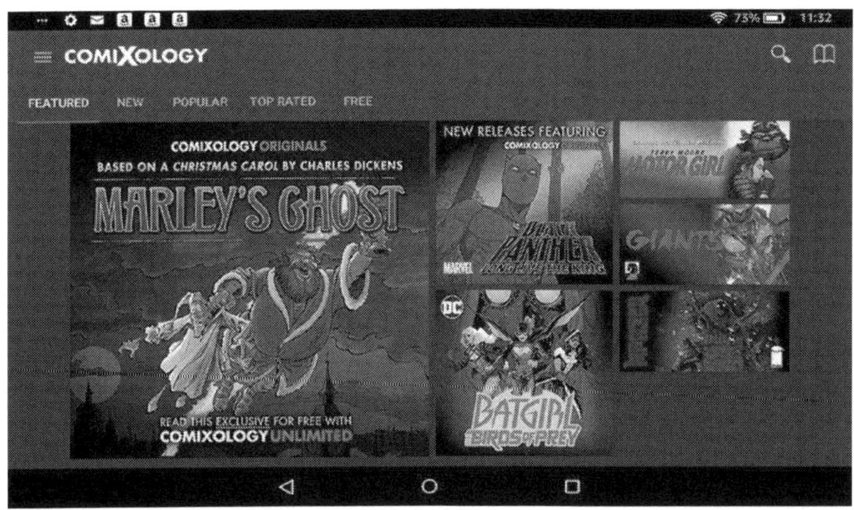

The Associated Press

This application is for one of the country's largest news organizations, the Associated Press. There information and stories often appear on the sites of other reporting outlets. This application allows users to get their information straight from the horse's mouth. With this application, you will be given headline worthy stories for your region or any selected region. You can also customize the content to cater to what you are most interested in and your geographic region. This app can be utilized in English or Spanish.

Autodesk Sketchbook

The Autodesk Sketchbook is an application for the artist in you. This is a pixel graphics application, which is intended for drawing and sketching purposes. It is a mobile art application which allows users to customize items at the drop of a dime. Users have the ability to pinch to zoom, use a variety of tools and brushes as well as organize your photo gallery. This even works with applications like Dropbox.

This feature works a lot like a mobile version of Photoshop. Users will need to create an account with the application in order gain access to more advanced features. These advanced features include tools like layering and even symmetry. A premium subscription is also an option which unlocks even more features and tools. This may include more brushes, selection tools and even advanced layering.

TuneIn Radio

TuneIn Radio is another free option for listening to radio and talk programs. This program is a free application which allows you to listen to more than 100,000 free radio options from around the world. This includes local radio, sports, news and even podcasts.

Feedly

Feedly allows users to see all of their pertinent news information in one place. With Feedly, you can organize, read and even share information. This application allows users to organize a variety of content. This content includes:

YouTube Videos

Blogs

Magazines

Publications

It also gives users a one-stop shop for all of the information they need. No more navigating to multiple sites for information. Feedly also offers integration with Facebook, Evernote, Twitter, Buffer, OneNote, LinkedIn and even Pinterest. Use the search panel to find and navigate to a variety of material and content.

Lastpass

Lastpass is the app for anyone who has a hard time remembering their passwords. It is used for storing and even generating your passwords. Lastpass also has the ability to autofill your passwords and logins on a variety of websites. Your master password will handle all of your other passwords. You also have the option to secure information like credit cards, photos and much more. Users can also store items like audio notes in order to set custom voice memos etc. It is also free to Lync across a variety of platforms with this application. This includes items on your Amazon device or even on your MAC or PC.

Evernote

Evernote, much like OneNote is a note-taking application which allows users to utilize advanced features not available through apps like notepad. With this application notes can be synced across multiple devices and items can be added to audio, video clips and pictures. You also have the ability to share, format and organize information. With the free version, you have the ability to upload 60MBs per month, any more than that and they would recommend upgrading to the paid pro version.

Trello

If you are looking for an app which can aid in keeping you organized and on your toes, Trello is just the app for you. It serves as a customizable bulletin board. It can be used to create notes, tasks and even to do lists. Bulletin board items can include pictures, text or even a mixture of both. Trello boasts a neutral design which allows for a variety of customization and changes. It can also even serve as an idea board for your personal ventures. The Trello application serves as an on the go project management suite. Trello even allows you to share your projects with others. You can invite friends to collaborate or work on your own. You even have the option of setting up workflows within the app.

Advanced Features and tricks of the Kindle Fire HD

Advance Your Carousel Interface

The carousel on your device is a staple for all Amazon tablets. Although there are some customizations which can be made, there are a few tricks to aid you in making it a little bit better. In order to remove items from your carousel long press the item, you would like to remove. You also have the option to long press and add items to collections, collections are folders/groups of similar items based on your discretion. This aids in keeping things more standardized and organized.

How to Install Another App Store

If you are a more advanced techie, you may wish to sideload another application store onto your Fire HD device. This can be completed the same way as downloading an ordinary application. However, you will need to find an APK file on the internet and download it to your device. Some notable apps include Slide Me as well as Get jar.

Using Your Quick Settings

Like many other mobile devices, the Fire HD 8 keeps the idea of quick settings alive. These allow users to access important feature without going through the full feature menus. In order to access these quick settings simply drag down from the top of your screen. There are several toggles like brightness and Wi-Fi. Some devices also have a Mayday option.

How to Take a Screenshot

If you are wondering how to take a screenshot, never fear, we will teach you. Screenshots are an integral part of any mobile device. In order to take a screenshot on your Kindle Fire device tap the standby and volume down button simultaneously. at the same time. The images will then be stored in your gallery.

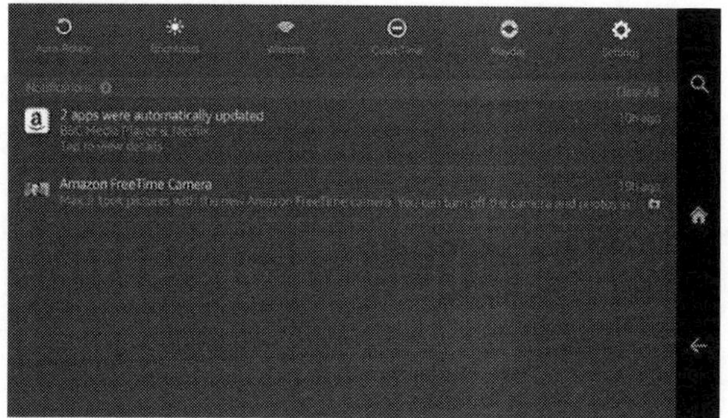

Adding Content to Amazon Cloud

If you didn't know, flash drives, CD-ROM and RAM storage are things of the past. Cloud storage is growing, easily accessible from any location and available almost anywhere. With your Fire HD device, this is no different. Amazon Cloud Drive is available to all Amazon users. This feature can be likened to dropbox, a place for storage of files, pictures, and various other document types.

Amazon Cloud storage is free but can start to cost depending on the size of the cloud you are looking for. For everyone, the first 5GB of storage is free. You also have the option of paying yearly fees for increased storage. Pricing may vary.

If you are looking to purchase a Prime Member ship, you will also get unlimited photo storage. This will free up space for a variety of your other files. For ease of uploading, use the Amazon Cloud Drive homepage. Once you are logged to with the associated Amazon account, simply utilize the plus sign in order to begin uploading. Once it is complete, it will be available via all of your Amazon devices.

How to Use Amazon Free Time

It's understandable for parents to be skeptical when giving their children full access to a device which is connected to the internet. Amazon Free Time aids users in getting over this dilemma. This feature is a profile which can be used for children and configured on your device to bundle kid content and applications. With Amazon Free Time parents now have the ability to create various profiles for their children. This will allow you to choose what content each of children will have access to and how long they can spend on specific area. This program allows your child to switch between various content like books and music all while browsing in an environment that is safe for them.

Before your child can begin to use this feature, you must successfully set them up with a children's profile. Please note that This enhancement will automatically block any access to social media features, location information and access to the Amazon store. It comes fully equipped with a browser specifically for children. In order to get started with this feature simply tap on the Amazon Free Time icon. It will potentially take a few moments to begin. It will then prompt you to create a PIN. This PIN will be used to exit the Free Time application. Once your PIN is created, you can create a profile for your child. Follow the steps shown below in order to begin creation.

If you are not currently in the area to begin immediate profile creation and navigating from the home screen you can begin this process by swiping downward from the top of the screen and selecting Settings. You will then need to tap **Profiles & Family Library**.

From this area choose Add Child Profile.

The first step in this process is simply adding the child's

photo. This is just an option and does not have to be completed. However, if you would like to do so simply choose to add a profile picture and select one from the device.

You will then be prompted to enter the personal information of your child. This will include name, age, date of birth and gender. You will then have the option to choose the age range for the child. This can be for children 8 and younger or a Teen Profile, for children 9 and older. The teen profile offers the normal look and feel of the Fire HD table but with updated security. Up to four profiles can be created within Amazon Free Time.

You will then need to update the content which your child has access to.

Once all of this is completed, simply tap Done for all of your profile updates and changes to be saved.

The child's profile will include a date of birth and even a picture if desired. Multiple children can also be set up on the device. Once this information is entered you will then have the option to choose what content, which you have already purchased, will be available to the child. Use the 'For Kids' switch in order for the system to display content which is deemed as Child-Friendly.

Once you have completed your choices, the display for your device will change. You will be shown a carousel view with only the items selected. The child will also not have access to the app store. No more worrying if your child is making purchases with your card.

Free Time will also provide your child with a simplified camera application. Whenever a photo or video is taken from within the child's profile, you will receive an alert. Parents also have the ability to restrict access to the camera.

Once everything has been created it can be accessed from the lock screen of the device. Once the profile is updated, you have the ability to alter a number of limitations. These include the following:

By Day: Free time allows parents the ability to specify various educational goals and place time limits based on weekend or weekdays.

Bedtime – You can also set a time for the device to be unusable. Select **Turn off by** in order to set the time where the device should be turned off. You can also set a **Stay off until** time, to specify when it can be used again.

Total Screen Time – This restriction limits the total amount of time the child can be in Free Time.

Time by Activity – This allows a parent to specify specific time limits for specific activities.

Getting the Most of Your Fire HD Storage

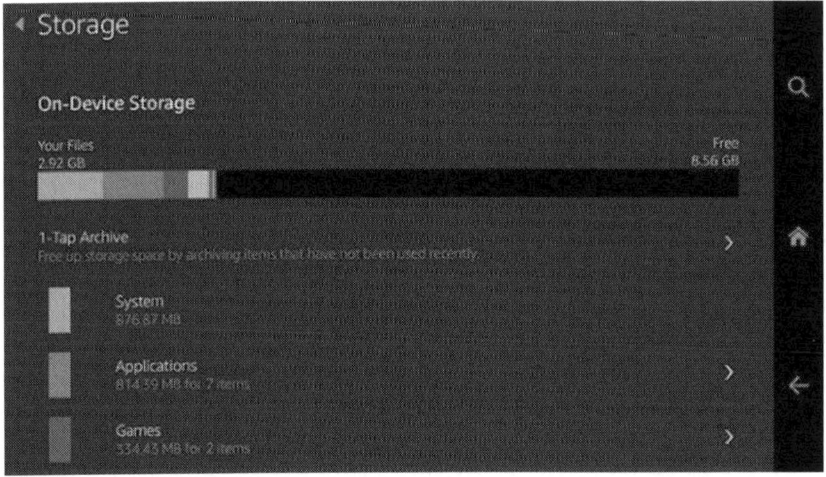

If you are ever running low on storage and you don't have the option of using a microSD card, use your settings in order to get the most of your storage. Navigate to the menu shown above by going to Settings on your device → Device Options → Storage.

This page will provide you with an overview of the amount of space you have used and free on your device. It will also show you the items which are utilizing the most storage space. A cool component of this page is the 1-Tap Archive. Tap this button and your device will determine what applications haven't been used in over thirty days and give users the option to delete them. Although they will be deleted from the device, you will have the option to redownload them again from the cloud area of your device.

Chromecast on your Kindle Device

Although Chromecast is not an item which is intended for use with the Kindle Fire HD, it can still be used. Due to the OS not including compatible software at the system level users must utilize a workaround in order to use Chromecast on this device. Your Chromecast can be used with your

Kindle device by using a Chromecast supported the application. These applications include Netflix and All Cast. All Cast can be downloaded from the Amazon store. It has the ability to be connected to the Chromecast and content can be beamed to the device/television.

Please note that initial setup of the Chromecast cannot be done on the Kindle Tablet.

6 Chapter – Troubleshooting & Common Issues

As you know our mobile devices will not last forever. They will also have issues which we may or may not be able to fix. This section will aid you in working with your device and troubleshooting common issues before you decide to trash it or take it to an expert. This chapter will provide the most common fixes to issues you may have with your device.

Purchasing Content Accidentally

Imagine having a child and being frantic because they have just purchased something on your device. You may have passed it to them without setting up the children's profile in order to gain some moments of peace. Whatever the reason, you now have a purchase which you do not want or need. Before passing your device off to your child make sure you set up a children's profile on your device. You will thank yourself later.

If you discover that the item your child has purchased, this will determine the eligibility for a refund. For Kindle books, returns may occur within 7 days of purchase. This will be handled through communication with Amazon's Customer Service team.

It is important to remember that certain Amazon Kindle content may be returned, however, purchases made via the Amazon App store or the Music store are nonrefundable. Amazon video purchase may also be canceled but have a shorter window. They must be canceled within 24 hours.

Setting Up Parental Controls

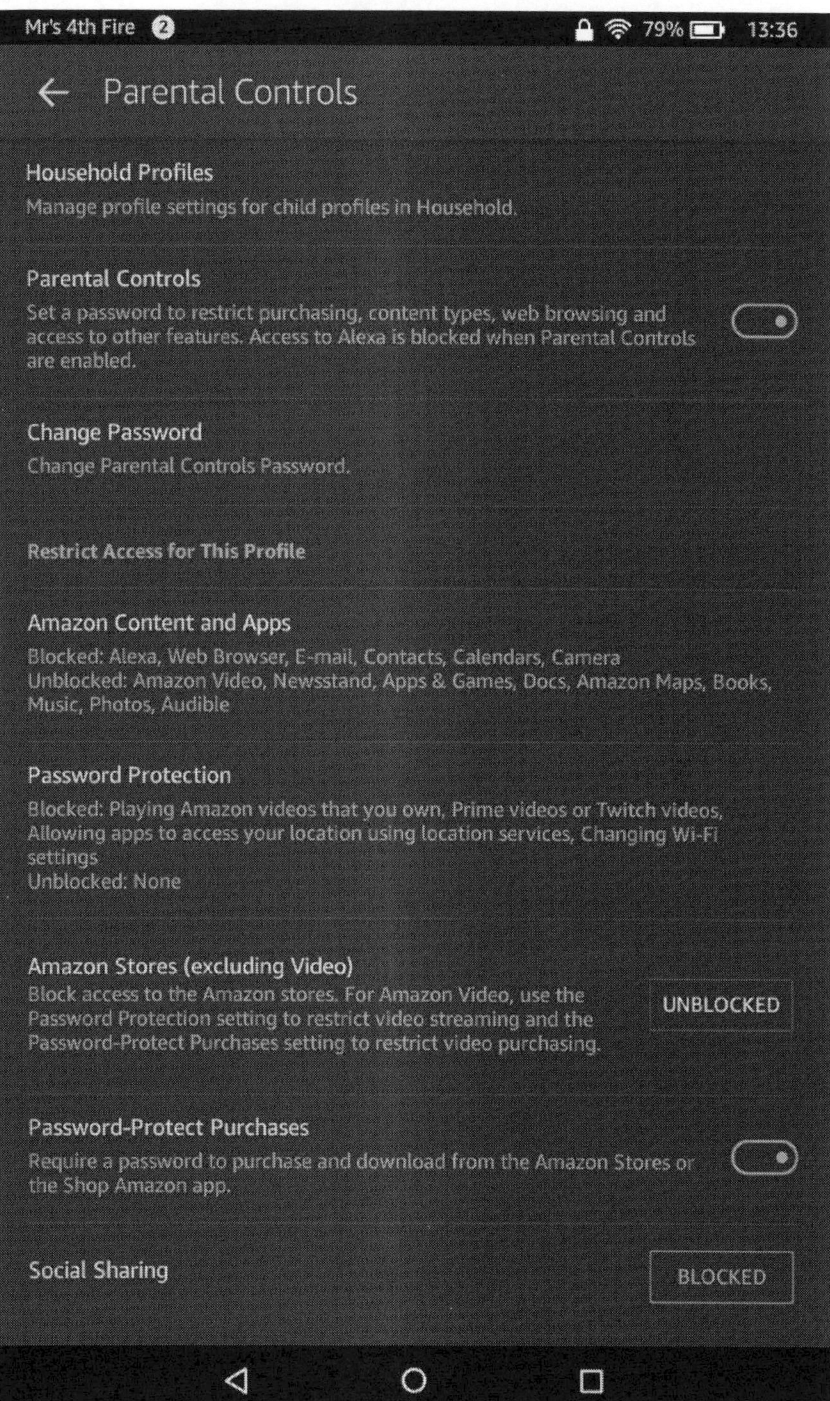

Mr's 4th Fire 2
79% 13:36
Parental Controls
Household Profiles
Manage profile settings for child profiles in Household.
Parental Controls
Set a password to restrict purchasing, content types, web browsing and access to other features. Access to Alexa is blocked when Parental Controls are enabled.
Change Password
Change Parental Controls Password.
Restrict Access for This Profile
Amazon Content and Apps
Blocked: Alexa, Web Browser, E-mail, Contacts, Calendars, Camera
Unblocked: Amazon Video, Newsstand, Apps & Games, Docs, Amazon Maps, Books, Music, Photos, Audible
Password Protection
Blocked: Playing Amazon videos that you own, Prime videos or Twitch videos, Allowing apps to access your location using location services, Changing Wi-Fi settings
Unblocked: None
Amazon Stores (excluding Video)
Block access to the Amazon stores. For Amazon Video, use the Password Protection setting to restrict video streaming and the Password-Protect Purchases setting to restrict video purchasing.
UNBLOCKED
Password-Protect Purchases
Require a password to purchase and download from the Amazon Stores or the Shop Amazon app.
Social Sharing
BLOCKED

Parental controls are an important an enhanced feature of your device. Amazon takes controlling what your children can and cannot do to a completely new level. This is all done through Amazon Free time.

The PIN or password you choose to use for your Amazon Free time access is different from the password used to get into your device. Once this password is created you can use it to manage a multitude of areas on the device and limit access and time spent on them. These manageable areas include:

The camera

Location Services

The Amazon store

Web browsing

Movies & TV shows on Amazon Video

Email, Contacts, and Calendar apps

Social network sharing

Wireless network connectivity

Specific content types (for example, Books or Apps)

You can also password protect one or more of the following:

Purchases from the Amazon stores on your device (for example, the Amazon App Store)

Once you have set up parental controls you will see a lock icon on the top of your screen. If needed one added bonus of the Fire HD device is the ability to add curfews. These can also be created to designate when a child can utilize the tablet. To set up a curfew you will need to tap **Curfew Schedule**. Once this is selected you will then need to pick the times and date which your child may utilize the device or when the curfew should take effect.

Unresponsive Touchscreen

An unresponsive touch screen can be one of the scariest items to troubleshoot because your device is essentially rendered helpless. The scenarios listed below are potential reasons why your touch screen may appear to be not working.

Your screen is frozen or not responding: This is the most common reason that your touch screen may not be working. To rectify this issue, simply restart your device. This can be accomplished by holding down the power button.

Screen is giving erroneous responses to touch: In order to rectify this Contact Amazon Customer Support.

Your touchscreen is damaged or cracked: If you find that your touchscreen is damaged or cracked beyond repair, contact Amazon Support for potential options. If none of these options are feasible there are a variety of shops and stores which will attempt to replace your screen for a nominal fee.

Press down on the power button and hold for 40 seconds or until your device restarts itself. Let go of the button once your device begins to be restarting.

In the event that your device does not restart press down your power button in order to turn it on.

Issues with Battery Life

If you are having issues with the battery life on your device, there may be something wrong. Follow the steps below in order to troubleshoot this further:

Charger is Not Properly Situated in the Device: Make sure that when charging your device your USB tips is secure in the charging adapter and within the device. Also, ensure that your plug is snugly fit into the wall.

Your Charger is Possibly Broken: A defective or malfunctioning charger may also be the reason that your device is not charging. Attempt to charge a different device with your charger to see if it works properly. You can also attempt to use another charger in your HD device to determine if it is working properly. If your device stays uncharged or the second device remains uncharged you will most likely need to purchase a new charger.

Your Fire HD Battery Will Not Stay Charged: If your device will not stay charged. Before attempting to do anything else, try to restart the device. If your battery does not stay charged, try using a different USB adapter. If your issue persists there may be a problem with your battery. If this is the case it will need to be replaced.

Wi-Fi Connection

Network connectivity is an important part of any Kindle Device being that they do not operate on cellular networks. Use the advice listed below in order to make sure that you are connected to the internet. Issues will persist if a wireless connection is nonexistent or weak.

Ensure your Wi-Fi is Turned On: A light cannot come on if you have not flipped the switch, the same goes for your wireless network. In order to ensure that your Wi-Fi is on navigate to the settings area of your device. From within settings, turn on the WI-FI. If your device still does not connect, hold down the power key in order to reboot the device.

WI-FI connection is weak: IF your device will not connect to the designated WI-FI your issue may not be the settings on your device. Double check your router and ensure things are working properly. If needed, contact your Internet Service Provider.

Forgotten Lock Pattern or Password

If you have forgotten the password to your device or cannot remember the lock screen pattern, never fear, there is a way to get back into your device. This can be achieved by setting your device back to factory defaults. This would erase all of the data on your device. If your reset does not work, Amazon support should be contacted.

No Sound Coming From Your Device

If you find that you are not hearing any noise from your device double check that it is not something you have done within the settings. In order to ensure everything is working as it should check the following measures below:

Your device's sound may be muted: If you are not receiving sound from anywhere on your device, the sound may be muted. To unmute your device, simply use the volume up button or change this within the settings. On your device, open settings and select 'Sound & Notifications'. Slide the volume bar to its desired position using your finger to unmute the device.

Your speakers are covered or damaged: In order to hear the sound clearly and without interference, make sure that your speaker is not damaged and free of any debris or other foreign materials.

Headphones are plugged in or connected via Bluetooth. If you are utilizing headphones to use your device make sure that the headphones are actually plugged in and operational. If you have utilized Bluetooth headphones, make sure that your sound is not still connected to the Bluetooth device.

Your Device Does Not Turn On

If your device does not respond when attempting to turn it on, this may be a matter of a dead battery. Start by simply plugging your device into the battery adapter. If your device still does not turn after the amount of time it takes to complete a full charge, verify that your charger is seating properly and indeed working. If your issue continues contact Amazon.

Issues in Connecting Bluetooth

If you are connecting to your Bluetooth and having trouble, there are a few things you can do in order to ensure that everything with your device is happening as it should.

Your Bluetooth is not turned on: Make sure that from within your Quick Settings menu the Bluetooth is indeed turned on. In order to make sure of this, navigate to your "Quick Settings", selecting "Wireless" and then selecting "Bluetooth". Tap "Enable" in order to begin locating the device or devices which you are attempting to connect to.

Bluetooth simply does not work: If the Bluetooth feature of your Fire HD 8 is turned on and still not working, you will need to ensure that the two devices are indeed compatible. Confirm that the Bluetooth is enabled on both the Fire HD and the device which you are attempting to connect to in order to ensure that he devices will properly pair.

Conclusion

If this is your first Kindle product, I hope you are wowed by what this device can do for you. If this is your first, I am sure it will not be your last. This guide only scratches the surface as to what you can do with your Kindle Fire HD 8. There is a world of possibilities out there.

The Kindle Fire was originally revealed in 2012, fast forward 6 years later and it is making strides we would have never imagined. These HD tablets are designed to keep you entertained and overjoyed. Watch movies, listen to music and of course read a plethora of great content.

The Kindle Fire 8 and its sibling the HD Fire 10 even offer Alexa in the palm of your hands. This makes them not only more durable but more efficient and effective than your regular old iPad. This is the 5th generation of the Fire and we can only assume that things will get better with time.

This guide is your how-to manual on using and getting the most from your device. If you ever feel like you need to re-read this information, it is always at your fingertips. What more could you ask for?

Don't forget – don't get the knowledge to yourself if you know a friend who struggles with utilizing their Kindle Fire HD 8, help them. Provide them with the same expert knowledge which you have just received from this guide. Are you looking to gift the Kindle Fire to your loved one? Include this guide as a supplement in order to get them started and get them on the right track?

Thanks for buying the book!

I hope you liked reading my book.

Made in the USA
Middletown, DE
10 December 2018